Anthony

THE D-DAY LANDINGS

The 100 day battle for Normandy

MEMORIAL
CAEN NORMANDIE

ÉDITIONS OUEST-FRANCE
13, rue du Breil, Rennes

Planning an invasion

◁ *Atlantic Wall bunker and beach obstacles.*

Sledgehammer and Roundup

When the Japanese attacked the US Pacific Fleet at Pearl Harbour in December 1941, the world's greatest industrial power became involved in the conflict, and at a conference in Washington the following month, Britain and America formed a joint staff and it was agreed that defeating Germany was the priority, but there remained basic differences between the two allies. The Americans wanted to relieve pressure on the hard-pressed Soviets by mounting a strong attack in the Pas de Calais region during the summer of 1942 (Sledgehammer), followed by a major invasion the following year (Roundup). The British preferred an attack in the Mediterranean, and their caution was justified in August 1942 when a large-scale commando raid on Dieppe was defeated. Apart from the fact that enemy submarines were still sinking more ships in the Atlantic every month than the Allies could build, there were not enough landing craft available for a large cross-Channel operation at that time. Instead the Allies agreed on a joint invasion in North Africa for November 1942 (Operation Torch), to be commanded by an unknown American general by the name of Eisenhower.

Casablanca and COSSAC

After the successful North African landings the Allied leaders met at Casablanca in January 1943, where they agreed to set up a planning staff known as COSSAC. Commanded by a British general, its task was to plan a full-scale invasion of Europe for the summer of 1944.

▽ *American wartime poster.*

American poster for war savings.

Although the submarine menace was still at its height, the tide was about to turn as the discovery of new radars gradually gave the Allies command of the vital Atlantic convoy routes. Bolero, the shipment of more than a million young Americans in a peaceful invasion of Britain began and the industrial might of the USA began to turn out the tanks, aircraft and weapons needed for victory. From headquarters in London the staff officers examined all the options, the first of which was the choice of where to land. The logical area was the Pas de Calais as that was the shortest route from Britain but was also the most heavily defended. The only other place with adequate beaches was the north coast of the Normandy between the Orne and the Vire rivers. This was at extreme range for fighter aircraft flying from Britain but its defences were correspondingly weaker.

The Willys Jeep - workhorse of the Allied armies in 1944

The Atlantic Wall

When Hitler launched his attack on the Soviet Union in the summer of 1941 he was forced to denude his troops stationed in the West and resolved to fortify the whole coastline from the north of Norway to the Pyrenees. That was a gigantic undertaking but work only started seriously in the summer of 1942 and was not finished by the time the Allies invaded. Essentially, the Atlantic Wall consisted of heavy gun batteries, infantry strongpoints, minefields and concrete bunkers, supported by a chain of powerful radar stations. The strongest concentration of defences was around the Calais area and the main ports such as Cherbourg and le Havre. The weakness of the concept was that it lacked depth and once the initial crust on the shoreline had been penetrated there was nothing further inland. The Allies were well furnished with plans of the fortifications, courtesy of the French resistance, and felt confident that a breach could be made. A further problem for the Germans was lack of troops to man the Wall and they had to resort to low-grade divisions made up of elderly men and in many cases, Russian "volunteers" who preferred serving in German uniform to starving in the prison camps.

The German situation

The supreme commander in the West was Field Marshal von Rundstedt, with 5,000 kms. of coast to defend, but his title was largely an illusion as Hitler in his distant headquarters controlled all important troop movements. In command of Army Group B positioned between the Scheldt and Loire was Field Marshal Rommel whose ideas on defence were diametrically opposed to those of his superior. Rundstedt preferred to let the Allies land and when he had determined the direction of their effort, to launch a massive counterattack with reserves based around Paris. Rommel on the other hand, believed that the only way to defeat the Allies was on the beaches as they landed, and when he arrived in January he began a massive programme of obstacles along his whole front. These consisted of minefields, barbed wire, wooden stakes and concrete tank traps placed between the high and low tide marks.

Field Marshal von Rundstedt on an inspection at Mont St. Michel.

Anti-aircraft gunners doing physical training with heavy shells.

Defending the Normandy area itself was the German Seventh Army with only four low grade divisions in the coastal defences which lacked motorised transport and were short of ammunition. Army Group B had only one armoured division in the area, 21st Panzer, which was based around Caen, and the armoured reserves could not be moved without permission from Hitler. That tangled chain of command was to prove fatal on the morning of D-Day.

The build-up of forces in Britain

The planned landing operations were destined to be the greatest amphibious operation ever undertaken and everything had to be calculated without the aid of computers. One major problem was the lack of experience of the fresh American divisions that were pouring in, and vast tracts of the countryside were requisitioned to form training areas. The British and Canadians too had to be brought to the peak of fitness before being moved south to prepare for embarkation. The entire southern coastline of Britain resembled a vast armed camp as roads were widened to take heavy tanks, advanced airstrips were built in open fields, stores depots were established and many kilometres of extra railway lines were constructed. In the harbours and estuaries the invasion fleet began to assemble, from several powerful battleships down to the thousands of small landing craft needed to get the men ashore. While all this was going

Flail tank, nicknamed the Crab. The chains rotated to explode mines.

on, small groups of very brave men slipped away in miniature submarines to undertake clandestine reconnaissances on the enemy coastline to study the latest state of the defences.

It was obvious to everyone that a major operation was planned: even to the Germans. What only a very small group of staff officers knew was when and where the landings would take place.

Engineering an invasion

The Dieppe raid had taught the staff officers a number of very important lessons. The first was that it would be extremely difficult to capture a major port with all its facilities intact. They therefore decided to take two prefabricated ports with them to Normandy, each the size of Dover. Codenamed Mulberry, they consisted of an outer breakwater of huge concrete caissons, and pierheads that rose and fell with the tide, linked to the shore by floating roadways. The various elements were built in Britain and towed across the Channel as soon as the landings were successful.

A second lesson from the disaster at Dieppe was that infantry on an open beach were very vulnerable and needed armoured support. The British General Percy Hobart was put in charge of a secret unit which developed a whole series of specialist armoured vehicles collectively known as "Hobart's funnies". The most important of these was a Sherman tank fitted with a waterproof "skirt" that could be driven through the sea by twin propellers. When it arrived ashore the skirt was dropped and it could operate as a normal tank. Other variants included a tank mounted with a flamethrower, various bridge-laying devices, a heavy mortar mounted on a tank chassis for demolishing concrete bunkers, and a flail tank with rotating chains at the front to beat a path through minefields.

In view of the huge numbers of vehicles involved the supply of petrol was of vital importance, and another group of engineers developed a flexible pipeline known as Pluto. The actual pipe was mounted on huge drums and unrolled as they were towed slowly across the Channel. Several such lines were eventually laid between the south coast of England and Cherbourg.

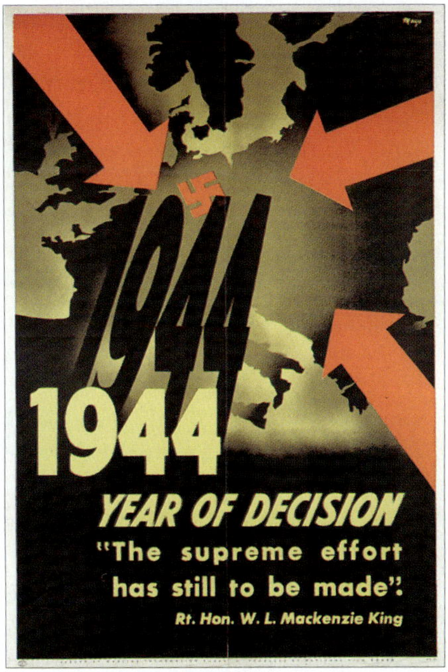

Canadian propaganda poster.

The Allied command structure and the plan

In view of the American preponderance in terms of men and material, General Eisenhower was appointed as supreme commander with a British deputy. The British also provided the air and naval commanders, and the veteran General Montgomery became commander of all ground forces for Overlord, as the invasion had come to be known. When Montgomery arrived in England at the beginning of January 1944 he was shown the latest version of the COSSAC plan for a series of landings in Normandy, and immediately stated his case for a much wider beach-head with more troops. That in turn created problems as there were not enough landing craft available which meant diverting vessels from the Mediterranean.

Montgomery worked hard to perfect the overall plan and presented the final version to the senior commanders in London on 15 May, after which the various staffs dispersed to their headquarters on the south coast. Overlord would start just after midnight on D-Day with airborne forces

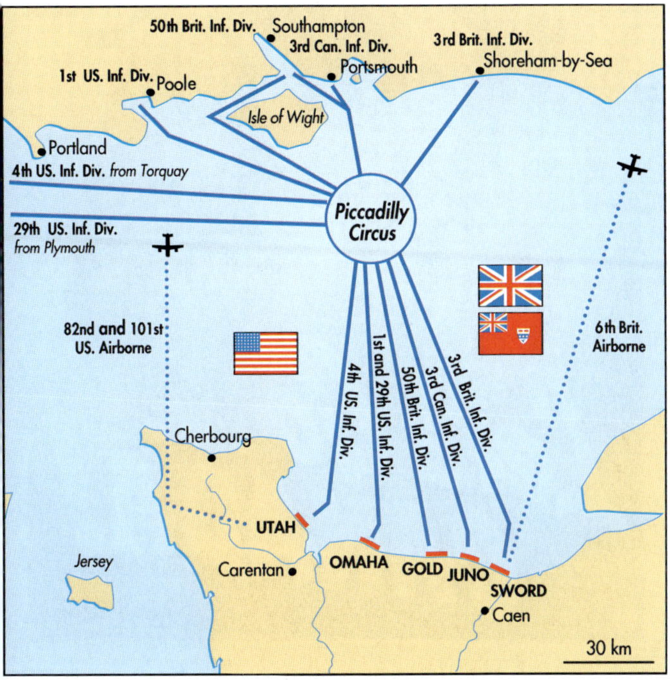

Map showing the embarkation ports and the routes for the convoys to the beaches.

landing to the east and west of the beaches. Their mission was to seal off the landing area against German reinforcements and secure vital routes inland for the troops who would arrive by sea. The next phase was a massive bombardment of the enemy defences by warships and aircraft, after which the first troops would step ashore at 06.30 hours. Running from west to east, there were five beaches selected, Utah and Omaha for the Americans and Gold and Juno and Sword for the Canadians and British.

All that remained to be done was a series of realistic exercises for the assault troops using live ammunition on beaches in England similar to the ones in Normandy. After that the men were moved into special camps near the ports of embarkation where they were finally told their destination and could study maps and photographs of the terrain they were to attack. All contact with the outside world was cut off and the only way out of the camps was on a landing craft bound for Normandy.

Fortitude - the deception plan

There was no way the massive build-up of forces in Britain could be hidden from the Germans and thus an essential part of the overall plan was to deceive them into believing that the landings would take place in the Pas de Calais. For that purpose a non-existent army group allegedly commanded by General Patton was formed in the Dover area complete with false radio traffic. Inflatable tanks, landing craft, and wooden replica aircraft were set up in the fields which German reconnaissance pilots were "permitted" to photograph - while being kept away from the real embarkation ports further west. When the real fleet set sail for Normandy, small ships towing large balloons were to steam up the Channel to deceive enemy radars, while the stations in Normandy would be jammed electronically to render them blind. Even well after the actual landings had taken place, most German commanders remained convinced that operations in Normandy were only a feint and that there would be an invasion in the Calais area.

Canadian propaganda poster.

Neptune and Overlord

Left to right. Air Marshal Tedder, General Eisenhower, General Montgomery. Behind : General Bradley, Admiral Ramsey, Air Marshal Leigh-Mallory, General Bedell-Smith.

Postponement

D-Day was originally scheduled for 5 June when conditions were regarded as ideal - a full moon for the parachute drops and a short period of daylight before the actual landings began combined with a low tide so that the enemy beach obstacles would be uncovered. Embarkation of troops and vehicles began four days earlier, by which time several of the larger ships were already at sea. By the 4 June, however, a veritable storm raged over the Channel and Eisenhower had to face the most difficult decision of his life. He finally decided to postpone the landings for 24 hours and after intense study of the weather charts his chief meteorologist predicted a short period of calmer conditions for 6 June. At 03.30 on Monday 5 June at the headquarters near Portsmouth, Ike as he was known, uttered his immortal words - "OK, let's go".

The departure

The maritime part of Overlord was known as Neptune, and Admiral Ramsay had a huge force at his disposal - 137 warships to bombard the German defences, 4,000 landing craft of various sizes and nearly 2,000 support ships. As the fleets sailed from every port

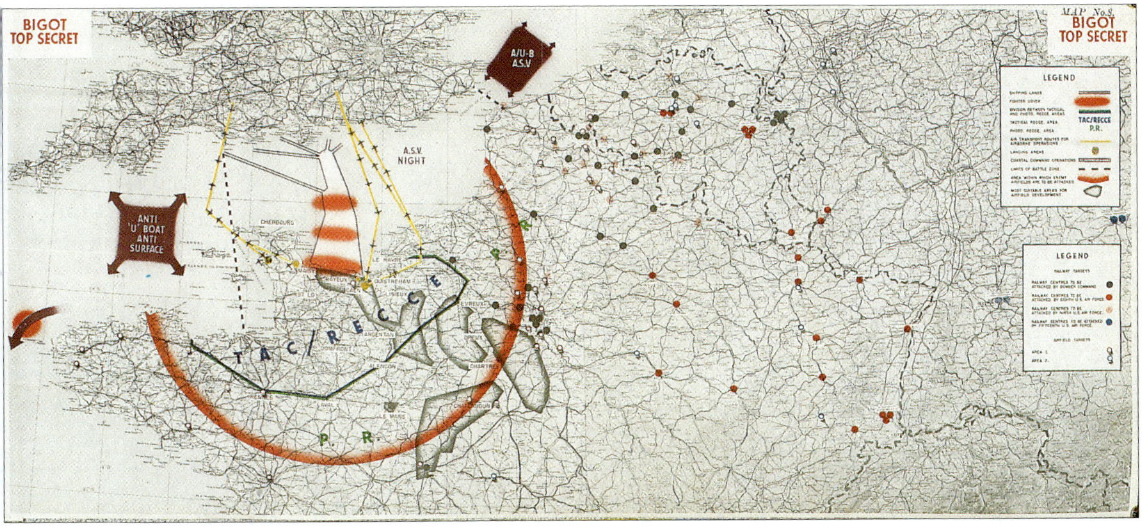

Map (extract) of the air force plan for D-Day. RAF reports.

EXTRA!
9 AM. FINAL Los Angeles Times 9 AM. FINAL
INVASION!
4000 Ships and 11,000 Planes Hit at French Coast
ENGLAND
LONDON
NETHERLANDS
GERMANY
BELGIUM
FRANCE
PARIS
LAST MINUTE INVASION BULLETINS
Special Invasion Edition

The first newspaper headline.

between London and Plymouth, the men on board knew that the long period of waiting was over and that this was not just another exercise. For most of them it would be their first experience of battle and the majority suffered the agonies of seasickness as the ships roll-ed in the heavy seas.

All the various convoys headed for a rendevous point south of the Isle of Wight, code-named Piccadilly Circus, from where they split into five task forces and sailed for their appointed sectors of the Normandy coastline, following the channels swept clear by flotillas of minesweepers. Overhead the Allied air forces patrolled the skies to make sure no enemy aircraft detected the passage of the fleet which arrived in position at around midnight, undetected by the enemy radars which had been effectively jammed.

Landing craft running in to Omaha Beach.

The airborne landings

As Admiral Ramsay's ships took up their positions some 15 kms. from the coastline, two large groups of transport aircraft carrying three divisions of paratroops were approaching. The first to arrive in occupied France on D-Day, however, were a small group of British commandos who crash-landed

Tank landing craft (LCT's) at Southampton just before D-Day.

British troops and their equipment inside a Horsa glider.

in five gliders at 16 minutes past midnight almost on top of their target, two vital bridges over the Orne and the canal between Ouistreham and Caen. Scrambling out of the wreckage of the gliders they ran for the bridges and rapidly overcame the startled defenders. Other special operations that night involved an attack on the heavy coastal battery at Merville and the demolishing of several bridges over the Dives to hinder the arrival of enemy reinforcements.

Insignia of the US 82nd Airborne Division.

Shortly afterwards the advance parties of the British 6th Airborne Division began to drop between the Orne and Dives rivers to secure the landing grounds for the gliders which would bring in more men and heavy weapons. The initial drops, however, were scattered and many men weighed down by their equipment drowned in the flooded marshes. But, when dawn broke, General Gale had set up his headquarters at Ranville and the division had established a strong defensive perimeter.

▷ British Airborne insignia.

At the other end of the beachhead, two US divisions, the 82nd and 101st, parachuted in to isolate the Cotentin and to secure the exit roads from Utah Beach. The Germans had flooded much of

▷▷ The US 101st Airborne Division insignia.

US Infantry coming ashore on Utah Beach.

the low-lying ground around the small town of St. Mere Eglise, which was the scene of an epic struggle before the Stars and Stripes was hoisted over the town hall at 04.00. The American parachutists were even more widely scattered and it took most of the night to collect the various regiments, but this did have the advantage of confusing the Germans who were getting reports of parachutists everywhere.

Utah Beach

Utah was the most westerly beach and the target of the US 4th Infantry Division. The German defences had been extensively damaged by a massive bombardment from sea and air. The first GI's landed at 06.30, supported by two squadrons of amphibious tanks which dropped their "skirts" and opened fire, much to the Germans' surprise. Engineers set to work to demolish the beach obstacles to enable the larger landing craft to sail in on the tide and discharge tanks and trucks while the troops flushed out the remaining enemy in the dunes. The problem with Utah was that the few exits from the beach were narrow roads over the flooded hinterland. Although a junction with the men of the 101st

◁ and △ *The insignia of the US 4th and 90th Infantry Divisions.*

After the men, the vehicles. Trucks making their way inland up one of the exits from Utah Beach.

Propaganda leaflet dropped from the air over Normandy on 6th June 1944.

The insignia of the US 1st Infantry Division, "the Big Red One".

Airborne had been effected by 13.00, more troops and vehicles were being brought ashore than could move off inland, and the result was terrible congestion. American casualties, however, were relatively light and their commander, General Bradley, could feel confident by mid-morning that the landing had been a success.

Omaha Beach

Omaha was a different story and confirmed Bradley's worst fears. There the terrain was different as behind the beach was a range of low cliffs into which the enemy had cunningly inserted their defences. In addition, they had recently been reinforced by an extra regiment, a fact which was unknown to Allied intelligence. Most of the preliminary bombardments missed the target and when the landing craft carrying the Ist US Infantry Division stormed ashore they were met by a veritable hail of fire. Those men who survived that took shelter behind the concrete sea wall, pinned down and unable to move forward. Almost all the amphibious tanks which should have supported them were launched too far out to sea and sank, leaving the infantry helpless. As wave after wave of landing craft swept in on the rising tide the congestion and the carnage on the beach became a nightmare, but with supreme courage, small groups of men began to move off towards the exits which were heavily mined.

At midday, General Bradley seriously considered abandoning the beach, but gradually his men succeeded in fighting their way inland to the coastal road where they began to drive

Insignia of the US 29th Infantry Division.

Troops struggling ashore at Omaha Beach.

the Germans out of the stone-built village houses. By the evening a tenuous bridgehead had been established and the beach finally cleared of the enemy.

As part of the assault on Omaha, a battalion of US Rangers was given the task of neutralising what was believed to be a heavy coastal battery on top of the cliffs of the Pointe du Hoc. Several of the landing craft lost their way, but Colonel Rudder and a few men succeeded in landing at the base of the cliffs which they had to climb. Under intense fire they made their way to the top where they had to fight their way through the complex of bunkers, only to find that the guns had been moved. Even so, they remained cut off for 48 hours and when relief arrived only 90 men were left capable of fighting.

The British beaches

Gold Beach was the sector between Asnelles and La Riviere which was the designated target of the 50th Northumberland Division. Owing to the appalling weather conditions it was decided not to launch the amphibious tanks offshore but to land them directly onto the beach. They were followed by the whole range of specialist tanks which were able to clear the mines, mop up the bunkers still resisting and place bridges where required, enabling the infantry to move inland fairly rapidly to secure the ridge of high ground behind the beach.

The 3rd Canadian Division at Juno Beach on either side of Courseulles faced a far harder task. Owing to rocks offshore they had to land when the tide was higher and many landing craft were damaged or sunk by hitting underwater obstacles. The Germans had fortified the villas and hotels along the beach and these had not been greatly damaged by the bombardment, causing delays as the troops attempted to move off inland towards their objective which was the main Caen to Bayeux road and the aerodrome at Carpiquet. Yet in spite of considerable casualties the Canadians managed to fight their way into open country and establish a solid bridgehead.

Sword Beach ran between the port of Ouistreham and Luc-sur-Mer and like Juno, was backed for much of its length by fortified villas. The 3rd British

Propaganda poster to include the French with the Allied troops.

Lord Lovat's piper playing the commandos ashore at Ouistreham.

Shoulder flash of the Canadian troops.

Division, however, supported by tanks and all the various "funnies", managed to clear out the defenders and open up the routes inland, not without having to cope with strong resistance. Accompanying the infantry were the commandos of the 1st Special Service Brigade whose task it was to clear the port and then move rapidly towards the canal to relieve their comrades who were still defending the bridges they had captured during the night. Among the commandos was a detachment of Free French commanded by Commandant Kieffer who assaulted the Casino at Riva Bella. Accompanied by his personal piper, Lord Lovat and his men arrived at the canal bridge at 13.00, a scene immortalised in the film *The Longest Day*.

The scene at Bernieres-sur-Mer on Juno Beach.

A gun emplacement on the Atlantic Wall disguised as a holiday villa.

The German reaction

Owing to the bad weather the Germans considered a landing extremely unlikely and were at a low stage of alert as well as being completely fooled by the Allied deception plan. Rommel was at home in Germany and the commander of the only panzer division in the area was in Paris with his chief-of-staff. The first reports which came in just after midnight spoke of parachutists landing, but the muddled chain of command ensured that no real action could be taken. When the landings started, the units along the coast did their best but except at Omaha were soon overwhelmed, and without transport were unable to regroup. The only German unit capable of intervening effectively, the 21st Panzer Division which was in the Caen area, remained paralysed by lack of orders, and when instructions finally arrived they were contradictory. One infantry regiment of the division was in contact with the British 6th Airborne to the east of the city but was unable to break through the British defence. It was not until the afternoon of D-Day that a battle group of light tanks from the division was able to mount a counter-attack to the west of Caen, aiming for the gap between Juno and Sword beaches. A few vehicles did in fact reach the coast but by then the assault troops were well enough established to beat them off.

Von Rundstedt remained convinced, as did Hitler, that the landings

Münchener Ausgabe

159. Ausg. 57. Jahrg. Einzelpreis 15 Rpf., 20 Rpf.

„Freiheit und Brot!"

Münchener Ausgabe

München, Mittwoch, 7. Juni 1944

VÖLKISCHER BEOBACHTER

Kampfblatt der nationalsozialistischen Bewegung Großdeutschlands

Invasion setzte zwischen Cherbourg und Le Havre auf Moskaus Befehl ein

So begann die Schlacht im Westen

Der mit aller Energie sofort aufgenommene Kampf unserer Wehrmacht gegen die Aggressoren ist in vollem Gange

Die Sowjetoffensive am Kanal

Von Helmut Sündermann

Starke Teile der Luftlandedivisionen vernichtet

Um Leben und Freiheit Europas

Es geht um die Entscheidung

Der Schauplatz der Invasion

Von unserem Marinemitarbeiter Erich Glodschey

The Nazi Party newspaper announcement that the battle in the west had begun.

in Normandy were a feint and refused to strip divisions from the Calais area to reinforce the crumbling front in Normandy. He did take the precaution during the afternoon, however, of ordering two further armoured divisions, 12th SS and Panzer Lehr to move towards the front, as well as several infantry units from Brittany.

The evening of D-Day

By nightfall the Allies had managed to land 130,000 men as well as the 22,000 parachutists for a total loss of 9,500 killed, wounded and missing - which was far less than had been estimated. The landing operations had been a tremendous success, but not all the initial objectives had been attained. To the east the British 3rd Division had failed to capture Caen and the Canadians hit stiff German resistance at the Carpiquet aerodrome,

△ ***Americans fighting in the ruins of a town in Normandy.***

◁ ***American soldiers and equipment on the evening of D-Day.***

although on the plus side, patrols had entered the suburbs of Bayeux. Royal Marine commandos landed on Gold Beach had cleared Arromanches, the site of one of the Mulberry harbours. In the American sector, the Omaha bridgehead was still precarious, and at Utah the infantry and parachutists were involved in a bitter battle with an elite German airborne unit for the vital bridges at Carentan which had to be captured before the two bridgeheads could be joined into a cohesive front.

Gaining a foothold

Montgomery's strategy

Monty's immediate aims were to join up the two American beachheads with those of the British, to get the Mulberries installed and then push an American corps west to capture Cherbourg. His main problem was one of logistics in that he had to get men and stores ashore faster than the Germans could reinforce the battlefield, and on 11 June he had sixteen divisions ashore facing fourteen enemy ones. In addition he had to keep the initiative and not allow the enemy enough time to concentrate for a counter-attack. His main advantage was total air superiority, and Allied fighter-bombers mercilessly attacked the two panzer divisions that were moving towards the front. The establishment of improvised landing grounds in Normandy greatly extended the range of the fighters, eventually forcing the Germans to move only by night or in poor weather.

Montgomery's essential strategy throughout the battle was to engage the German panzers in the Caen area to enable the Americans to cut off the Cotentin and then move south towards Brittany.

Servicing and re-arming a Spitfire on an advanced landing ground near the beaches.

The American sector

The battle for the bridges at Carentan was a costly one fought in the flooded marshes, and the town was not captured until 11 June, thus enabling the junction of the Utah and Omaha beachheads. Bradley had two essential tasks - to move south to take the road junctions of Coutances and St. Lo, and west to capture Cherbourg. Fighting their way over the floods to the south of St. Mere Eglise, the GI's succeeded in crossing the Cotentin to the south at Barneville on 18 June, thus cutting off all the German forces in the Cherbourg peninsula. At the same time, another army corps launched an attack from Carentan towards St. Lo, which soon ground to a halt in the Normandy bocage country.

Americans moving inland into the Normandy bocage country.

The bocage problem

The bocage which covers much of Normandy consists of small fields surrounded by high banks and ancient hedgerows which proved to be perfect terrain for defence. The small narrow sunken lanes proved quite unsuitable for tanks which could easily be picked off from the hedgerows, and the campaign rapidly deteriorated from one of movement into small infantry units advanc-ing a few metres at a time. The Ger-mans fought courageously for every field and could not be easily dislodged by air

The hedgerow problem. A patrol trying to attract fire from a German sniper.

Tank reinforcements in the ruined port of Cherbourg ready to move to the front.

attack. Yet until the Allies had driven the Germans out of the bocage country they could not break out into the more open terrain south of Caen and make use of their armoured divisions.

The capture of Cherbourg

Having cut off the Cherbourg Peninsula, General Collins was able to turn west towards Cherbourg which Hitler had ordered to be defended to the last man. Again the Germans contested the advance but by the evening of 21 June the Americans had arrived on the hills overlooking the harbour. There they were faced by a series of concrete bunkers which had to be reduced one by one before moving down the narrow defiles into the town. The Germans began to demolish the harbour installations but on 26 June the key to the defences, the Fort du Roule, was captured. The garrison commander surrendered to the Americans but resistance from some of the forts on the outer mole continued for a few more days. Cherbourg was the only port in Normandy capable of handling large ships and thus was a vital prize, but it was not until early August that the Allies were able to use it effectively.

The British sector

In keeping with his general strategy, Montgomery was determined to keep the German armoured division pinned down in the Caen area, while at the same time attempting to outflank the city. The airborne bridgehead to the east was too narrow for exploitation, so he ordered the commander of the Second Army, General Dempsey to attack to the west. The failure to take Caen on 6 June was a costly error and the Canadians found themselves engaged around Carpiquet by elements of the 12th SS Panzer Division. Dempsey's men fared little better as the attempt to take Tilly-sur-Seulles was blocked by units of the freshly arrived Panzer Lehr Division and

A Panther tank belonging to the Panzer Lehr Division near Falaise.

Mulberry Harbour caissons during construction in England.

The wreckage of the Harbour at Arromanches after the storm.

A map showing the consolidations of the five beach-heads and the capture of Cherbourg.

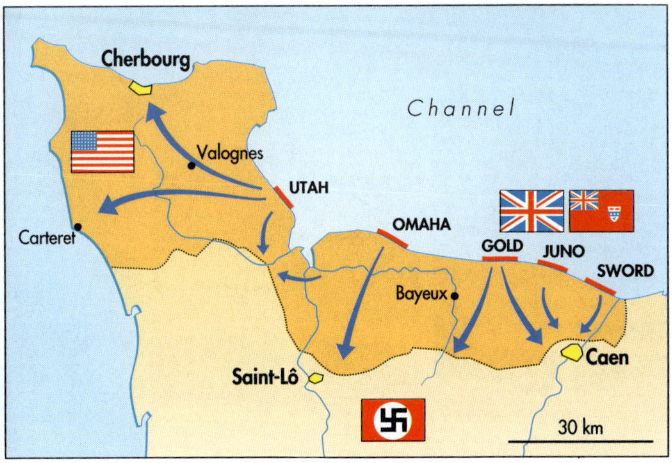

the 7th Armoured Division was driven out of Villers Bocage. On 13 June the offensive ground to a halt with little territory gained, giving the enemy a vital breathing space to bring in reinforcements and establish their defences.

Logistics

The first elements of the Mulberry harbours began to arrive on 7 June and two were constructed, one at Omaha Beach and the other at Arromanches. Both were more or less finished by the 18 June but during the following three days, disaster struck. A violent storm all along the coast totally demolished the one at Omaha and severely damaged the other at Arromanches. The latter was repaired and rendered valuable service, but the storm was a terrible set-back for Montgomery in his efforts to build up his forces more rapidly than the Germans could reinforce. He was constrained to conserve stocks of ammunition and petrol until such time as he had enough to mount another major offensive.

Stalemate

The defeat of Operation Epsom

Montgomery planned to recommence the offensive on 23 June by attacking with three divisions to gain a bridgehead over the Odon to the west of Caen and advance towards the Orne. The storm, however, caused a delay in bringing in fresh forces and he was unable to start until five days later. In the meanwhile, the Germans had succeeded in bringing in strong reinforcements and by the end of the month had eight panzer divisions in Normandy. Once again the weather hindered the deployment of aircraft, but after a heavy artillery bombardment, the infantry managed to force crossings over the river in the pouring rain. On 29 June the 11th Armoured Division managed to capture the strategic Hill 112 and held it in spite of German counter-attacks, but Dempsey believed that the enemy response was much stronger than it actually was. He made the decision to pull his tanks back behind the Odon, enabling the Germans to recapture Hill 112, and the offensive degenerated into a battle of attrition. The British had lost 4,000 men and in spite of seriously damaging the enemy units, had suffered a serious defeat.

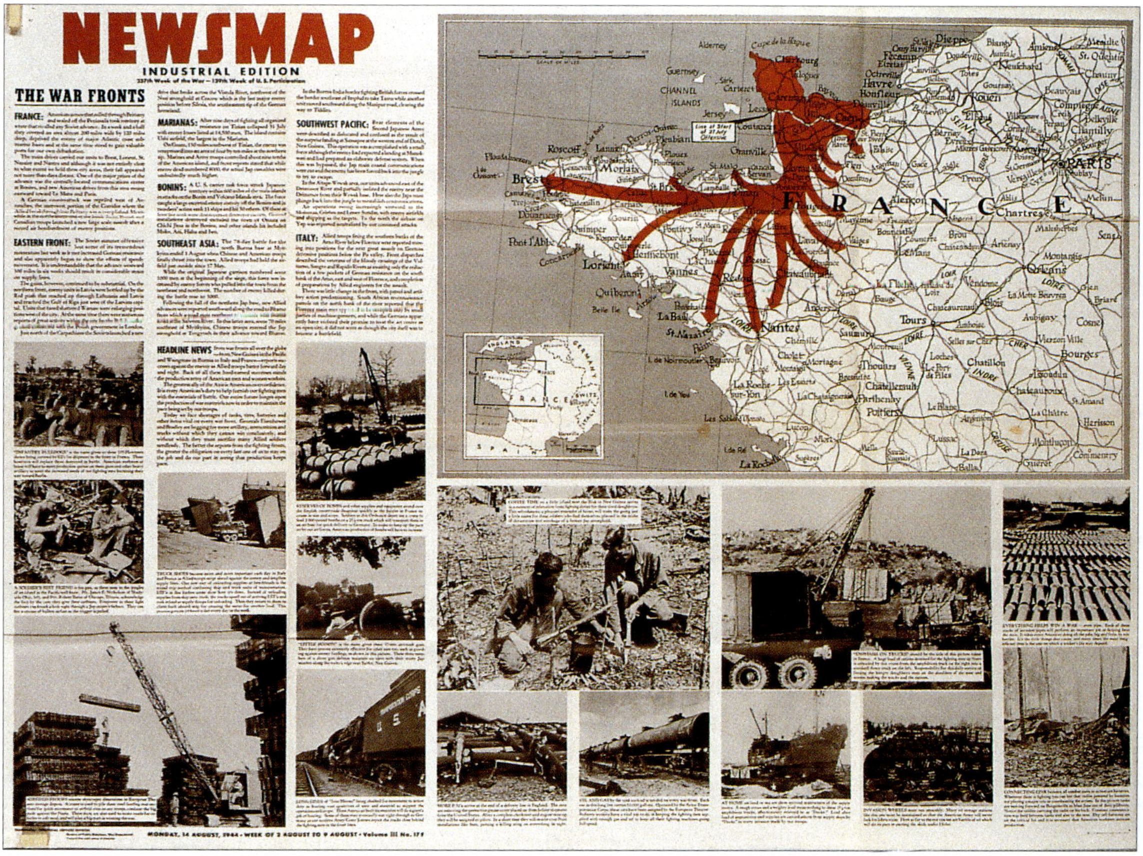

An Allied information poster illustrating the development of the American break-out after Operation Cobra.

The Americans in the Bocage

Having taken Cherbourg, Bradley turned his attention to St. Lo which as the hub of a vital network of roads, had to be captured. On 3 July he launched a two-pronged assault, pushing four divisions towards La-Haye-du-Puits and a similar force down the road from Carentan to Periers. Although the German divisions facing the Americans were relatively weak, they conducted a spirited defence in the bocage and the flooded valleys. In spite of American superiority in terms of air support and artillery the attack ground to a halt on 10 July although they did manage to take La Haye. Bradley threw in fresh troops and the terrible battle of attrition lasted for a further nine days until the exhausted GI's took possession of the smoking ruins of St. Lo.

American jeeps driving towards the ruins of St. Lo.

Operation Charnwood

While the Americans were suffering in the bocage, the British launched a major offensive designed to clear the enemy from Caen, hoping to gain the open country to the south towards Falaise. On 3 July the Canadians attacked the 12th SS around Carpiquet, supported by the guns of a battleship and swarms of fighter bombers. In a three day battle both sides suffered appalling casualties in the ruins of the aerodrome until the SS finally retreated over the Orne.

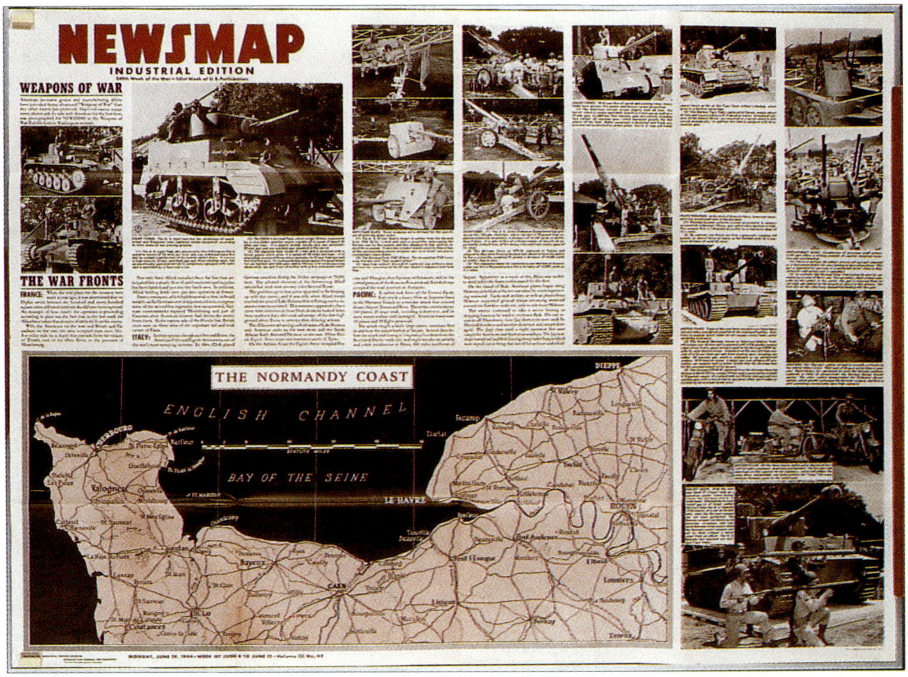

An Allied poster showing the coast of Normandy and some of the weapons used.

Caen in ruins after the bombardment.

The capture of Carpiquet cleared the way for a frontal assault on Caen which started with a massive air bombardment on the evening of 7 July which devastated the historic city. For two days the infantry struggled through the ruins but were only able to take control of the northern part, with the enemy remaining firmly entrenched south of the river Orne. Although Montgomery claimed that he had won a great victory he had not achieved his objective, except insofar as he had engaged all the enemy armoured divisions and kept them away from the American front.

Thousands of people in the city were homeless.

The Allied situation

In early July the American press began to openly criticise Montgomery's conduct of the campaign claiming that he was too cautious and that his tactics were costing American lives. On the battlefield the situation was one of virtual stalemate in that the British had still not achieved enough space to manoeuvre and the Americans were stuck in unfavourable terrain. The Germans, however, had suffered high casualties and Montgomery was well

▽▷ *Field Marshal von Kluge conferring with senior officers.*

▽ *Propaganda poster of a soldier and a member of the resistance fighting the same battle.*

aware that many of the panzer divisions were little more than regiments. The enemy defences would eventually break and it would be he who determined where. In spite of the often vocal criticism, Montgomery remained calm, arguing that his strategy was correct. His immediate aim was for the Americans to consolidate along the St. Lo to Periers road, prior to launching a massive attack towards Avranches and Brittany. At the same time and in conformance with his general plan, the British would clear the southern parts of Caen and advance towards Falaise.

The German dilemma

On 2 July, von Rundstedt was sacked by Hitler for suggesting to the High Command that they make peace and replaced by Field Marshal von Kluge. Four days later the commander of panzer troops in Normandy was also replaced and on 18 July Rommel was severely wounded in an air attack on his car. Changes at the top, however, made little difference to the conduct of the battle. The Germans had conducted a magnificent defence but the tide was turning in the Allies' favour. Hitler's insistence on hanging on to every square metre of territory had forced the German commanders to throw in their panzer divisions to plug holes in their front rather than massing them for a counter-attack, and Allied air superiority had severely hindered their ability to resupply. Logically the enemy should have shortened their line by retiring behind the Seine, but any talk of retreat was anathema to Hitler. As Montgomery gathered his forces for a final breakout into open country, there was plenty of fight left in the Germans, but their defeat was inevitable by mid-July.

Operation Goodwood

While the Americans mopped up the last defenders of St. Lo and fought their way forward to the hills overlooking the St. Lo to Periers Road, Montgomery planned another offensive to pin down the German armour around Caen. His aim was to launch three armoured divisions on a narrow front east of the city to gain possession of the Bourguebus Ridge which dominated the road to Falaise. On the evening of 18 July, a massive bombardment by aircraft and warships was meant to obliterate the enemy defences, but when the tanks set off they were brought to a rapid halt by the effective German anti-tank guns. The offensive ground to a stop and all that Montgomery had to show for the heavy losses was a successful Canadian offensive to clear the southern suburbs of Caen. Back at Eisenhower's headquarters in England there were demands for Monty to be replaced, but that was politically impossible.

Preparations for Cobra

Cobra was the codename for the American breakout which should have started on 20 July, but Bradley was forced to postpone it owing to constant rainfall. As his men formed up along the start-line he was faced with 30,000 Germans but only one armoured division, Panzer Lehr. In reserve, ready to exploit the break-out he had General Patton who was due to take command of the US Third Army on 1 August. On 24 July there was yet another postponement owing to the weather, but the orders came too late to stop a fleet of bombers already in the air. A huge carpet of bombs was dropped but many missed their target and hit the American lines causing severe casualties.

Breakout

◁ *A parish priest wearing an old steel helmet rescuing his belongings.*

Cobra

In spite of the appalling weather Bradley gave the go-ahead on 25 July and after yet another massive bombardment the GI's advanced across the St. Lo to Periers road. The initial combats were indecisive but on 27 July, the thinly stretched enemy line broke and General Collins discovered that the way was open for his tanks. Bradley then pushed Patton through with a stong armoured corps which raced west towards Avranches leaving any opposition to be mopped up by the infantry. They reached the town on 30 July, captured the bridges intact and without stopping, broke out into Brittany. Other units headed for Le Mans and the Loire as the campaign was finally transformed into one of movement.

▷ *An American column near Coutances after the break-out.*

Operation Bluecoat

For Mongtomery it was imperative to support Bradley's left flank and to engage the enemy divisions south of Caen. He ordered the Canadians to clear Bourguebus Ridge to open the road to Falaise and the Second British Army to mount a major offensive west of the city towards Vire - Operation Bluecoat. On 30 July the British attack started but was slowed down by strong enemy resistance still in the bocage country. Even so, Beny-Bocage was captured and patrols pushed into Vire, forcing the Germans to start a gradual retreat as the Americans were already threatening their rear areas. Montgomery was disappointed by the slow progress of the attack and sacked a corps and an armoured division commander.

▷▷ *A British "Tommy" in the ruins of a Normandy village.*

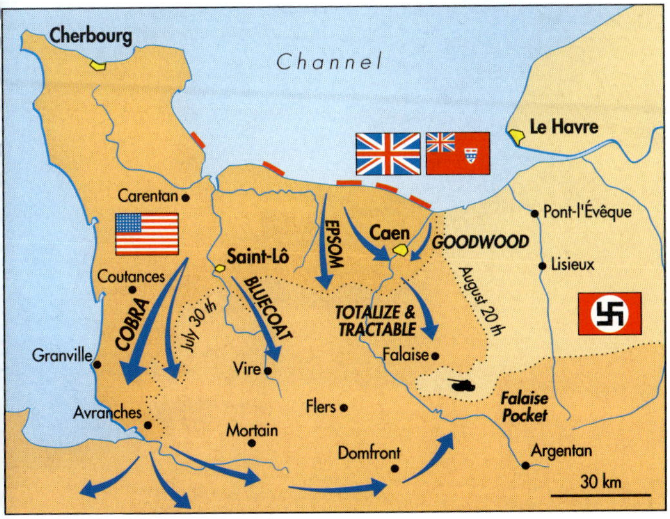

▽ *A map showing how the move to entrap the Germans at Falaise was developed.*

The last gamble - Mortain

In his distant headquarters Hitler could see that Avranches posed a serious threat to his whole front in Normandy, and on 2 August, ordered von Kluge to assemble a total of eight panzer divisions to cut Patton's lines of communication. Kluge, who would have preferred to withdraw the rest of his forces behind the Seine was forced to comply, but owing to British pressure could only extract four divisions with only 250 tanks between them. Protected by low cloud the Germans moved into position for an attack on Mortain, but Bradley was aware of what they were planning and positioned his forces to block them. On 7 August the enemy attacked in thick fog and made initial gains of some 20 km, but at midday the weather cleared and the thickly packed columns of tanks were easy prey for the fighter-bombers. Soon the lanes were choked with burning vehicles as the survivors tried to extricate themselves from the chaos.

It was then that Bradley saw the chance to inflict a total defeat on the Germans in Normandy and Montgomery agreed his plan. With the enemy off balance, Bradley directed part of Patton's army to move north from Le Mans to get behind them. At the same time the British would advance towards Falaise as the other jaws of the pincer that would catch the Seventh German Army in a massive trap.

The price of failure. tiger tanks destroyed at Mortain.

The Caen Falaise road

By the end of July the Canadians had achieved the status of a full army and their task was to force their way south to Falaise. With most of the enemy armour engaged at Mortain, Operation Totalize started on 7 August after yet another massive air bombardment. Initial progress was quite rapid but the enemy reorganised and managed to establish a new line of defence. If he was to close the gap and meet up with the

Canadian Sherman tanks waiting to move towards Falaise.

▽▷ *The corridor of death. The remains of the German Seventh Army.*

▽ *A Canadian convoy in the ruins of Falaise.*

Americans, Montgomery had to move quickly and on 14 July he launched two armoured divisions southwards towards the Dives over which the Germans were already starting to escape. On 17 August the Canadian infantry entered the ruins of Falaise while the Americans were approaching Argentan. It was then that the Allied commanders began to worry about their forces bumping into each other and in a decision which remains controversial, the American XV Corps was ordered to halt.

Closing the trap

By 16 August 100,000 Germans were starting to stream through the 30 km. gap between the Allies and across the Dives towards Vimoutiers and the Seine. The following evening part of the Polish 1st Armoured Division managed to seize the crest of Mount Ormel which overlooked the valley and in the clear weather the fighter-bombers inflicted terrible carnage on the densely packed German columns. All the small lanes leading down to the river were strewn with wrecked vehicles and the bodies of men and horses. It was not until 22 August when the Poles and the Americans met at Chambois that the Falaise pocket was finally sealed, officially ending the Normandy campaign. The enemy left behind most of their vehicles, ten thousand dead and fifty thousand prisoners, yet 20,000 did succeed in slipping though the Allied pincers to fight another day as a result of the last-minute slow down of the attacks.

Conclusion

The 100 days of the Normandy campaign saw a major Allied force established on French soil and poised to liberate the rest of the country, in conjunction with the troops landed in the South of France on 15 August who were advancing up the Rhone. D-Day itself had been an immense success but thereafter the combination of difficult terrain and poor weather had hampered the Allied effort. In spite of the criticism heaped upon Montgomery it is difficult to see what else he could have done until both the British and Americans could free themselves from the bocage which was defended with great skill by a tenacious enemy. The Battle of Normandy took a final toll of 240,000 Germans killed or wounded, 210,000 prisonners, 1,500 tanks and 3,500 guns destroyed. Two German armies had been annihilated including one armoured. The path across France was opened at last.

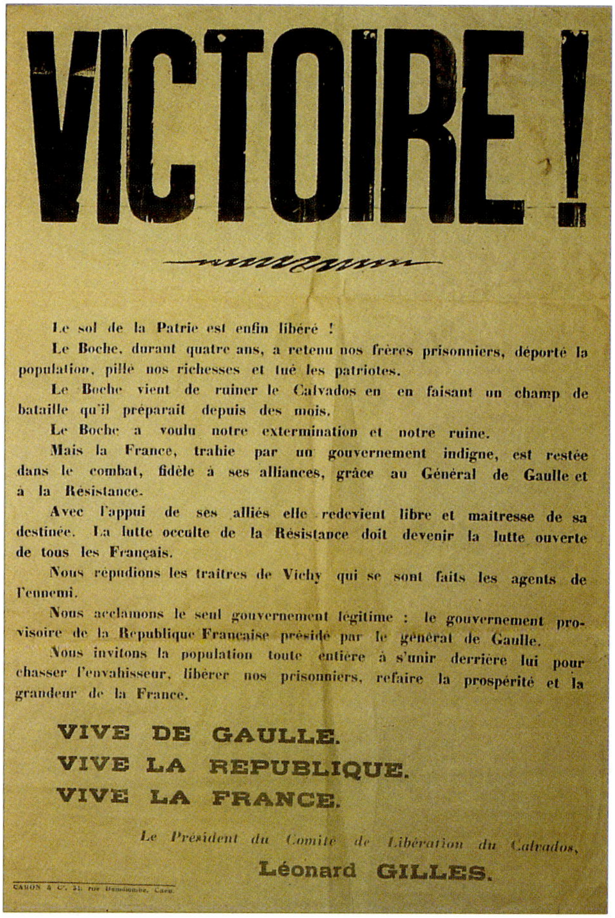

VICTOIRE !

Le sol de la Patrie est enfin libéré !

Le Boche, durant quatre ans, a retenu nos frères prisonniers, déporté la population, pillé nos richesses et tué les patriotes.

Le Boche vient de ruiner le Calvados en en faisant un champ de bataille qu'il préparait depuis des mois.

Le Boche a voulu notre extermination et notre ruine.

Mais la France, trahie par un gouvernement indigne, est restée dans le combat, fidèle à ses alliances, grâce au Général de Gaulle et à la Résistance.

Avec l'appui de ses alliés elle redevient libre et maitresse de sa destinée. La lutte occulte de la Résistance doit devenir la lutte ouverte de tous les Français.

Nous répudions les traitres de Vichy qui se sont faits les agents de l'ennemi.

Nous acclamons le seul gouvernement légitime : le gouvernement provisoire de la Republique Francaise présidé par le général de Gaulle.

Nous invitons la population toute entière à s'unir derrière lui pour chasser l'envahisseur, libérer nos prisonniers, refaire la prospérité et la grandeur de la France.

VIVE DE GAULLE.
VIVE LA REPUBLIQUE.
VIVE LA FRANCE.

Le Président du Comité de Libération du Calvados,
Léonard GILLES.

Posters proclaiming the victory in Normandy and the liberation.

Photographic credits

SHAA : p. 2 (top). **BDIC** : p. 2 (bottom). **T. JULLIEN** : p. 3 (bottom). **MEMORIAL DE CAEN** : pp. 3 (top), 4, 5, 9 (top), 10 (top left), 11, 12 (middle and top right), 13 (middle and left),15 (middle), 17, 18-19, 20, 21, 23 (middle), 24, 25, 27, 29 (left), 30, 32. **Mémorial/M. Seyve** : pp. 7 (top), 8, 9 (bottom), 10 (top right), 14. **IWM** : pp. 6, 11(top), 15 (top and bottom), 23 (top), 26, 29 (right), 31 (right). **ARCHIVES NATIONALES DU CANADA** : pp. 10 (bottom) PA-133757, 31 (left) PA-115570. **DITE** : pp. 12 (top left and bottom), 13 (bottom), 22 (top). **BUNDESARCHIV** : p. 16. **ECPA** : pp. 22 (bottom), 28.
The cover is made up of documents on pages 7, 11, 14 and 15.

Cartography : AFDEC, Paris

I.S.B.N. : 2.7373.2105.0 - Dépôt légal : juin 1996 - N° d'éditeur : 3493.04.06.12.00
Technic Plus Impression, Betton (35)